How to Get Your Ex Back

Dude You're Gonna be Mine AGAIN!

The 4 Weeks Foolproof Program to Assess Yourself, Get Him Crawl Back to You and Keep the Fire Burning

JOSHUA CLETIS

CONTENTS

Outline

Some relationships last for eternity, but most partners breakup after dating for a while. People split up for various reasons, with some being extreme and with others being due to minor issues that were left unsolved by two unwilling individuals. The dating realm can often be frustrating.

Breakups are scary. Your world can come crashing down when you part with your significant other. The reality can hit you like a tidal wave, and you realize that you are never going to mean to this person what you meant to him some time ago. The sheer heartbreak sends waves of regret and longing throughout the body.

Maybe that's you right now. If you are reading this, chances are that you can hardly tell if the guy you want is interested in you. Besides, there is a reason why you broke up. You are in a vulnerable and confused state. You miss the feeling of loving and having someone in your life who cares for you and supports you in every way. You have countless memories stored in special places in your heart and mind. The remainder of how that special man once made you feel is still fresh.

You needn't worry, though. A breakup does not have to be permanent, and reuniting with your partner could be one of the most rewarding things you experience in your life. The intimacy and dependency you'd built with your ex do not have to go to waste. Also, reuniting does not have to imply that you or your partner are desperate. It could mean that you are willing to put all your differences behind you, forgive each other, and begin on anew through mutual growth and efforts. If the man you lost was the companion for you, it is important to look beyond the causes of your breakup and your differences and try to get him back.

It is never too late to make the right moves. You really want him back, but that's clearly the reason you are making so many mistakes and strengthening his reason for staying away from you. You have to understand that the more mistakes you make, the less your chances of getting him back are.

This book includes a secret code that guides you every step of the way in getting your ex back. It shows what a man really wants from a woman and how to make him decide to give your relationship another shot. It does not comprise of anything like sexy dress code or whispers in the ear to capture his instant attention. If you are willing to be patient, this book is perfect for you. It presents you with a four-week program to ensure you get your love back for good. It provides you with ways to use the rational part of your brain to obtain a clear perspective on your relationship and how you can lead your man back to you.

Inside this book, you will be guided on:

- The different perspectives of love, dating, and relationships between men and women

- How to understand if the lost one was really the one for you

- The mistakes to avoid when trying to get your ex back

- How to perform a personal assessment and understand yourself better

- A four-week program of the activities and steps you need to take to get him crawling back to you

- How to improve yourself and be attractive to him

- How to keep the fire burning after getting him back

- Key secrets for a healthy relationship.

Introduction

Most people struggle with thoughts that they could have established a great and lasting relationship with their ex. These thoughts preoccupy their minds and consequently inspire funny behavior around their ex. While they think they are capturing their attention and making them regret leaving, they keep giving their ex a reason to stay away from them all the more while hoping they will return. The biggest enemy to solving things with a partner who you are in conflict with is trying too much whilst the both of you stand on two different grounds. People realize that they lost a gem because they could not understand what their partner really wanted, and they didn't know how to attract them back into their lives. Also, most women do not seek to understand if the man they really want to recover was "the one"; hence, they spend a good part of their life wondering where they went wrong and why their ex-boyfriend never wanted them back.

It is good to understand that some breakups are for the better. Peace is one of the most precious gifts you can allow yourself in life, and you do not need a partner who you can't click with, let alone sail through life with. For you to start attracting your ex back into your life, there is a need to perform a self-assessment and realize if you still need him back and if he is actually a good match for you. There is also a need to be tactful as you try to capture his attention, since you might be doing the wrong things altogether. Therefore, you might want to know what men really want from a woman and how to achieve that.

Remember, being in a relationship with someone who actually believes in you, loves you, inspires you, motivates you, and looks out for you can be a gateway to happiness. In one way or another, we all need love. As humans, if we did not need love, then the population would include fewer people, and we would perhaps be living on private islands; however, it is innate in humans to want to love and be loved. It gives us the drive that we need to walk through all the valleys and hills in life. However, there is a big difference between being in a relationship for convenience and being together with someone you really love. For others, the companionship is just great and better than the involvement of deep emotions. After all, we are living in a difficult world where such convenience matters for your happiness and other activities in your life. This emotional attachment or convenience relationship could be exactly what you are looking for in your ex, and that's perfectly fine.

Not all hope is gone. Maybe the separation is what you required for the both of you to realize that you need each other. There is a great chance that with the right attitude and actions, you can get your ex back. The rest of the book will guide you through tactical steps that, when followed, will ensure that you don't drive your partner away for good. They'll help you get him back and keep him forever.

Thank you so much for choosing this handy guide for getting back your ex. I hope you'll enjoy this reading so I'll be glad to hear for your thoughts with a short review on Amazon.

SECTION 1: ESTABLISHING WHETHER YOUR EFFORTS ARE WORTH IT

***

Chapter 1: Different Perspectives from Men and Women on Love, Dating, and Relationships

One interesting thing about human nature is that men and women view the world from different perspectives in so many ways. Research shows that all of us want to have everything. We tend to attach a similar sense of significance to most aspects of life, including career, work-life balance, and wealth (Rossi, 2018). Especially in a liberalized world where men and women are free to choose to do anything, everyone often strives to acquire the best. Most interestingly, both men and women have feelings, but they tend to express them differently if they choose to express them at all.

Ideally, both genders have unrealistic views about stuff, and relationships are not an exception. This often becomes a source of conflict between two partners who are unable to compromise on their ideas and perspectives. If only there was an exit interview for every relationship that ended, then the difference would be easy to understand. However, if we listen to most people who have parted ways, one thing we are sure to hear from them is that their partner didn't understand them or that their partner didn't care about the fact that they needed something in particular.

Understanding these differences and appreciating this beauty of nature as a woman can be the best weapon for dealing with a man in any context. You can build meaningful relationships with a lot of ease, and you can learn to appreciate the different needs that your partner has rather than just following them to see that your own needs are met. As shown below, the basic principle herein is that men and women have different points of view concerning relationships.

Importance attached to sex and the implications of behavior for both men and women

We have been brought up to believe that sex is good and a God-given way of embracing the oneness of a man and a woman. Furthermore, sex has been used to measure the level of commitment and intimacy in other areas of the relationship through its presence or lack thereof. Sex is good when each partner feels wanted and can get vulnerable with their partner. Its importance in a healthy relationship cannot be underestimated. However, the different views about sex between men and women lead to some expectations that, in turn, cause frustrations and misunderstandings.

We should learn to appreciate the fact that God used these differences to make men and women complement each other. Men's orientation is that sex indicates physical cohesion; it is a high priority and it should include variety. Women believe that sex is a sign of emotional cohesion, and they may not consider it to be a priority. For these women, it is not physical but relational. Consequently, men are mostly roused by the sight of a person they consider sexually appealing while women are stimulated by the sense of touch, words, and the attitude of a man. For men, any time can be a good time to get sexually active. Women go through cycles where they desire intimacy at times and they don't at other times. Also, a man concentrates on sex, and they do not think about other things during sex, while the woman is easily distracted by other things going on in her life.

Furthermore, for a man to connect sexually with a woman, they want to feel physically needed, admired, and respected. A man will not want to be let down by a woman, lest their ability to connect sexually with them is reduced. On the flip side, a woman will need to feel emotionally desired, given a man's time, and feel loved to be able to connect sexually. Clearly, sex in the relationship is a man's way of expressing love. They tend to put more emphasis on it more than women do, and even if they may not show it, men feel connected to their partner in this way, which meets most of their needs.

A man will tend to fuss about the physical side of the relationship, because it is directly linked to their self-image. If the woman is showing reluctance, the man is tempted to think that the woman does not appreciate his physicality and takes it as a sign of rejection. Sex lies at the epitome of the self-esteem of a man. On the other hand, the woman needs the relationship more than the physicality and the reason for her reluctance may be caused by unresolved disputes between them. Therefore, sex is one of the things that determine whether relationships last or break because of the differences therein. Overall, sex is a powerful tool for connecting two people in a relationship. It performs magic that only a few other things can.

Importance attached to emotions and implications on behavior

As mentioned earlier, it is masculinity and femininity that men and women bring to the table which provides the relationship with a good balance. Women and men have different attitudes toward the emotional side of the relationship. Women have a dire need to feel loved and accepted by their partner. A woman needs to feel safe and secure emotionally. She needs to share intimate conversations with her partner. She needs to hear gentle words of assurance from her partner and also to be set apart from the rest. She does not expect that any other person is loved better than her.

Also, women typically demonstrate their emotions. They often share every emotion, because for them, it is a therapeutic technique to relieve anxiety and stress. Whatever a woman is feeling tends to reflect in their behavior, body language, and facial expressions. Most importantly, most women tend to judge men by how emotionally attached they prove they are to them, hence they fall for the words that men use. A woman will mostly assume that her actions are enough to show her man that she has a problem, without necessarily asking for help directly. She will leave it upon her man to understand her need for help, and if he does not, this comes off as not caring enough. At times, men may not recognize the problems their partners are going through; hence they appear to be emotionally unsupportive. Also, men tend to overlook the emotions of their women and fail to dig deeper and know whatever is going on. They may not recognize the kind of emotional support a man needs if the problem is not spoken about directly. Even if they realize the problem, men will give instrumental solutions while women will expect an emotional and empathetic solution.

Men, on the other hand, tend to mask most of their feelings. Although this is somewhat human nature where sharing emotions does not bring men similar satisfaction as women, men consciously and subconsciously respond to long-established societal standards. Due to this reason, men will have fewer friends that ladies do. Even for the few friends that they have, men will hardly confide in their friends. They choose to use their friendships for doing stuff such as playing games. Also, they do not get the kind of emotional support that ladies often give each other.

As a woman, you will realize that your close friends call up to check on you and even ask you how you and your partner are doing. It is easy to confide and let out any bitter feelings you may be holding for your partner. However, men do not get this from fellow men. Their friends will mostly call to ask if they can do business, play video games, go clubbing together, or participate in other such activities. This does not mean that men never want to confide in someone; it is just difficult for them to identify someone to confide in.

As a result, men will mostly solve emotional problems on their own. It is hard for them to admit that they need help. They strive to be objective in all situations and obtain solutions for their concerns without leaning on the emotional side. Also, men will hardly tell you that you have annoyed them. They will watch to see how your behavior toward them progresses to ascertain if they are respected and admired for their masculinity. They opt to not fight battles for which the solutions cannot be found; signs of disrespect can hardly be cured. This is the same way they handle conflicts at work or in other fields, so such responses are not limited to your conversations and arguments. A man will choose to withdraw and not bombard you with questions. On the flip side, women often take conflicts very personally and invest a lot of their emotions in a single situation.

More so, a man studies the behavior of his partner and how they react to things they try to open up and talk about. If they cannot deem it good to confide in you, then they will develop an emotional distance between the both of you, which can be detrimental to your relationship.

Aspects to focus on to get your partner back

So, you have the utter longing to get back with your ex. You have already realized that men and women have inherent differences in how they handle various things in a relationship. For instance, a woman will get emotionally attached and begin to visualize a lifetime with their partner, because they feel like their love is forever. On the other hand, a man will be physically attached and will be looking forward to when you are meeting next so they can attain a sense of fulfillment for being around his woman. He enjoys her company and does not rush things, because his emotional attachment grows over time depending on how compatible he is with the woman. Ideally, a man will be initially attracted by the physical compatibility he has with a woman while a woman will first be attracted by the love she feels for a man and also how she feels loved by the man.

However, each man is unique in their own way. What works for one may not work for another. This creates the need to establish a point of view of your ex. Hence, one of the major things you should focus on is understanding his weaknesses and beginning to visualize how these can be addressed. Although it is not possible to change someone, you can always influence change, which has to come from within if it is to last. As noted above, men have a difficult time showing their emotions. As such, you must be focused in avoiding judging him by the words he uses with you but instead by how much he enjoys being with you. You must be ready to take his greatest weakness and turn it around to be a pillar of your relationship. Focus on knowing his greatest deal breakers. Remember the things that people used to do to him that would annoy him and those that made him happy.

Realize that men do not handle multitasking well in the manner that you can as a woman; you can always engage in a conversation around a serious issue and cook or catch up on the news at the same time, but men cannot do this. Men like to handle one task at a time, while women juggle between tasks and attain good results. With this knowledge, you will realize when and how to talk to your man.

Most importantly, recognize that in every woman is a power that, when well leveraged, can help them get the man of their dreams. Therefore, focus on the reasons that led to the breakup and assess yourself to see if you are ready to compromise.

Chapter 2: The Starting Point in the Recovery Process

Now that you are more knowledgeable about how men perceive love, dating, and relationships, you most likely have formulated new ideas about the subject. There are some aspects that you failed to consider or that you did not consider while you were in the relationship. This is essential and determines your next move as to whether you still want to have your ex-boyfriend back. It requires you to think with clarity to make a good decision. Be honest to yourself as to what you want and how you feel about your ex-boyfriend. It is ideal that you do not act out of desperation; be sure that this is what you truly want.

Reasons that led to the breakup

You feel that this is the person you want to spend the rest of your life with. Also, you feel that you can still try and be sure that it was not meant to be. To be honest, you need to revisit the reasons that you and your ex-boyfriend broke up in the first place. As noted, there are some cases where relationships end because of simple mistakes that would have been addressed but you were too proud to solve them. You may be the one who was too proud to listen to be humble or accept that they made a mistake. However, there are instances when what came in between you both is so significant that it may not be in your best interest to get your ex-boyfriend back into your life. Some of these reasons are detailed below.

He was a narcissist

The people you should avoid getting back with are the toxic types, such as a narcissist. You should not want to get back into a relationship with a person who abused you physically and/or emotionally. Even if you get back with them, they will almost certainly continue with their abusive behaviors. In fact, they will be eager to take advantage of the fact that you brought yourself back to them. Therefore, they will accept you back easily and shower you with love, only for their traits to come out eventually and bite you in the back.

Cheating

One of the most painful reasons for a breakup is cheating. This is more of a betrayal, and most especially people in a serious relationship experience tremendous pain. You may be the one who cheated, in which case things can be a bit tough for you to get your ex-boyfriend back. You will have to do more to prove that you are now a person of character. The truth is that men do not handle cheating in the same as women. While it is easy for a woman to forgive a man who cheated on her, it is not the same case for men.

Also, it may be your boyfriend who cheated on you and felt betrayed such that you had to end the relationship. In most cases, when it comes to women, they can blame themselves when their partners cheat on them. For instance, they will feel that they are not beautiful, intelligent, or giving the relationship enough. For men, it is more of an attack to their self-esteem, and they feel that their partner disrespected them. The issue with cheating is it kills trust, and this is vital for the relationship. If he is the one who cheated, you have to first understand that cheating is a personal decision, but that there are motivators of cheating which you might have contributed to. For instance, if you were always insecure, you may have not been able to get really intimate with him, and he eventually met someone who sparked that fire in him and made him feel appreciated as a man. Nonetheless, lying even about the simple things can hurt both of you. Therefore, dishonesty is something that may have put you or your boyfriend off.

Lack of support

One of the basic ingredients of a successful relationship is support for one other. Especially in the contemporary world, we are experiencing various changes and have to handle a lot of things, so we all need a shoulder to lean on sometimes. Therefore, you may have broken up because you were not supportive of your partner. Maybe he would be stressed, and you acted like it was not worth your energy or time.

Being supportive is a vital aspect of keeping a relationship. Also, maybe you feel like you lacked the emotional support that most women crave. However, you have now learned that this mutual support is gained through compromise and the willingness to communicate openly to balance each other's feelings. Therefore, you might be willing to try being a more supportive partner and be ready to listen and encourage them in their endeavors.

Remember, support for men goes a long way in showing them that you believe in them and the dreams that they have. They may not be at a stable place career-wise or financially, and this may be causing most of the frustrations they experience. Your place is not to criticize them or pretend like it does not concern you. It is about pushing him and cheering him on. If you can't be your man's biggest fan, then you can't expect your relationship to be healthy. Also, you are now willing to speak out and not demonstrate your emotions, expecting them to read your mind and respond to your problems.

Lack of passion and affection

The truth is, affection is a basic ingredient of a successful relationship. The reason as to why you broke up could be because you were withholding attention and affection. It may have happened that you were not affectionate with the person, and then he stopped asking for the affection. If a person is turned down enough times, it becomes embarrassing to ask. Remember that affection is not about only sex. It may be simple things like cuddling on the couch, holding hands, or other forms of attention. Surprisingly, these simple acts tend to add intimacy in a relationship. When you withhold this affection from each other and are not willing to keep the fire burning, the relationship stops making sense, and the next logical thing to do is to break up.

You may have broken up because your ex-boyfriend had misdirected anger, and he would always retract whenever he was bothered by something. For instance, maybe he had a bad day at work and comes home in a bad mood. Normally, even if a person had a bad day, they will be eager to come home, hug you, and tell you all about it to get the right attention. Despite the fact that men like to handle emotions alone, you could offer a hand to hold for your partner, and he does not have to act like you do not exist. However, now you know better. You know how to give him the space he needs and not take it personally. You know how to differentiate between when he is moody because of you or other personal things, and as the sober person, you will know the right way to hold his hand and keep the affection. Among the major mistakes women commit is that they think every time a man is angry or moody, it's all about her, and she responds with withdrawing and eventually affection is decreased.

Clashing values and lack of compromise for each other's values

Another possible reason as to why you may have broken up is your clashing values; this is a major basis for conflicts. Maybe this led to giving up because one of you was not ready or willing to compromise. Poor communication or silence in the relationship may have made either of you assume things rather than communicating to establish a common ground. However, you may have taken communication out of hand by nagging. This is something else that puts off someone and they get fed up with it. This is especially the case if you are always willing to be heard and not to hear out your partner. As with other reasons for a breakup, this too goes both ways. He may not have been a listening partner and you kept repeating the same issue over and over without really solving a thing. It is upon you to establish if it is possible for you to find common ground when you get back together.

Most importantly, these factors can be contributed by either you or your partner. It is good to establish who caused the breakup among both of you. If you clearly contributed to the breakup, you have a great task ahead to show them that you are worth their time. You have to convince them that you are a better person who is willing to make it work. (This is discussed in detail in the four-week program below.) Sadly, even if he is the one who led to the breakup, he might not be in a position to ask for your forgiveness. He might believe that you were fed up with him and opt for moving on with his life. Therefore, it is on you to show him that you still want him, but be ready to make it clear that such past behaviors will not be tolerated.

What you know about them now

After looking at the reasons why it did not work out, which could include one or more of the reasons noted above, you have to look at your ex-boyfriend. The question you are seeking to answer is whether it is possible to get him back. It is more important to really take a look at them to know what they are doing with their life and their status. Do not confuse this with stalking, because the latter is not only illegal but will hinder your efforts to get him back. The reason for looking him up is to know whether he got married or if he is engaged or in a serious relationship. If either is the case, it will be quite challenging to get them back. Furthermore, the odds are against you, because your ex-boyfriend will think that you are coming back now because they have someone else, so it may be interpreted as jealousy. You will not uncover all the details by just looking them up, but you should be able to gather enough information to do what is needed.

It is important to note that sometimes the idea of wanting to have them back may come from within you. It is not that you came across them, but that you feel they are the person for you. You have to ask yourself how long has it been - weeks, months, or years? What could have changed in their life in that amount of time? Did they gain or lose a job? Do they move out of the country or state? In some cases, what happens is that you may have left them while they were unemployed only to realize that they now have a good job. In certain cases, especially if they feel that you left because they were lacking in money, it will be a task for you to prove how you truly feel about them. However, if you are determined, you will eventually win.

It is important to note that at this point there is no contact with your ex-boyfriend. So, you cannot ask them how they are doing, about new things in their life, or if they are seeing someone else. There are some cases that are surprising in which you will learn that immediately after you left, they got with someone else. This could be a rebound relationship that they entered hoping to get over you. So to know the current status of your ex, you may want to check their social media pages. People tend to update what is happening in their lives on different social networks. You should look through it without commenting or liking their posts or images. This is a constructive use of social media where you personally and soberly look him up with a clear objective, and that is to know his current status, where he is, what he is doing, and, most importantly, whether he is approachable.

Going ahead with the recovery

At this point, you have done your best to assess the situations necessary to determine whether you will continue with the recovery. You have uncovered what has been going on in your ex-boyfriend's life; remember that this is not stalking, and the fact that you were able to avoid the temptation to like their images, posts, or comment means that you are ready. It is about being a different person and objective for that matter.

There are various things going on in your mind right now. There are questions you have, one of which being whether you will choose to move ahead with trying to get your ex-boyfriend back and whether he will be willing to forgive you. Will he love you again? At this point, you may be scared, and you may be worried that your ex has moved on completely. At this point, it can be termed as closure, because you have to deal with trying to move on. However, it is good to be optimistic; besides, if he is the one for you, there is a need to know his side of the story.

Chapter 3: Self-Assessment

Importance of self-assessment

Self-assessment is one of the keys that open the gateway to successful relationships in any setup. Self-assessment ensures that you know and understand yourself better than anyone else. Whilst it may be a relatively difficult task to undertake, the rewards for the task can be great. It greatly improves the chances of having a more successful relationship than you have had in the past.

There are various self-assessment tools online, thanks to the high amount of content on the internet. Most of these tools are free, and they can help you discover things about yourself you may have never known. You find that people with a low self-awareness know very little about the knowledge that others have about them that is unappealing. In the case of preparing to recover a relationship and make it work, there are four important areas you will need to assess yourself on. These include emotional maturity, physical wellness, social balance, and financial wellness. We delve into these topics in detail below.

Emotional maturity: This is perhaps the most important test you will take. It helps you find out if you are carrying any baggage from the past, including the heartbreak that you endured when you split with your partner. It helps you establish if you have mastered the art of controlling your thoughts, which ultimately determine your moods and attitude. Additionally, it helps give you direction, because you want to achieve a life that you desire in the near future.

- **Physical wellness:** This is also important in recovering a relationship, because the first step in gaining confidence is accepting and appreciating your own body. It helps you to understand if your eating habits and exercise programs are satisfactory and what you might need to do as you take on the four-week program.

- **Social balance:** This is an important aspect that reduces over-reliance on a partner. You don't want to get back with your ex with a messed up social life lest you put too much strain in the relationship. Like it or not, certain senses of fulfillment are only achieved through connections with other people outside the relationship. As a woman, you have a special strength in relating cordially with other women. This strength enhances the special intimacy you might share as a couple, and it might just be what your ex-partner needs.

- **Financial wellness:** We have heard countless times that finances are among the worst enemies in a relationship. Whilst this is not always the case, financial problems have led to several relationship breakups. This part helps you put all credit generating fields of your life under control. You don't have to necessarily be stable in your career, but you should ensure that you won't over depend on your man for all financial needs. Be ready to contribute and supplement their efforts with what you bring to the table. Times are hard, and every man needs a woman who does not rely on him for everything.

One of the most important questions you can ask yourself while conducting a self-assessment is if you would be satisfied with you if you were to date yourself. You might be relaxed believing that you are this irresistible gem with wonderful traits and features, but care to ask yourself why your partner left; he may not be thinking of getting back with you, and you might have simply fed your mind with a beautiful image of yourself that isn't real.

Self-assessment helps you realize if the person who left was good for you and whether you were good for him. Could it be that your hidden traits came between your relationship and made it fail? Could it be that you have already established that your ex is ideal for you, but you lack the appropriate mental image of yourself?

Mind you, self-assessment is not only important for people who seek to get their ex back into their lives. Psychologists recommend self-assessments from time to time in a relationship, to account for the constant changes that people experience. Seek to understand if relationship issues greatly destabilize your joy and tranquility.

Without good levels of self-awareness, our automatic response to conflicting situations is to blame everyone but ourselves. We tend to accuse others of the negative attitudes and feelings. The truth is, you have the power within you to maintain a healthy relationship by taking charge of it, and your partner can always follow. Even without their awareness, you can take charge of the relationship and begin the recovery process to make it stronger than it was before.

After understanding your traits, ask a selfless question of if you would be happy being with a partner that behaves just like you. Some are selfish when approaching a relationship, and they cannot endure a kind of behavior while being deluded to imagine that their partner would bear it from them. Unfortunately, this flawed thinking does not apply in the real dating scene. There is that need to evolve beyond the traits that aren't so lovable.

Self-awareness can help you to improve yourself substantially until you are confident in agreeing that you would love and be in a relationship with someone like yourself. This improvement is going to inspire a shift in your ex-partner. They will realize a sense of emotional maturity, self-control, and originality. Of course, assessing and improving yourself does not mean that your ex-partner does not have to work as well. Part of making your ex come back to you is being calm, composed, and asking for what you need without anger or selfishness. It means that you have taken the deliberate move to improve your interpersonal relations. Nobody loves being in a relationship with someone who does not get along well with people.

Finally, understand that the beauty of human nature is enhanced by our imperfections. Do not expect that you can get all the pieces of your life to be intact before beginning to pursue your ex-partner. You only need to have a reasonable level of each of the important aspects discussed above to be successful in your mission.

Do you need him back? Do you still love him?

At this point, you have already established the reasons that led to your breakup, and you probably also have an idea of where he is in life right now. You now realize that it is viable to go ahead with the recovery process, and you've conducted a self-assessment to understand what aspects of yourself you may have to improve. With a deep understanding of the key aspects of your life, you can easily establish if you still love him or the exact reasoning for wanting him back.

If you suspect you haven't quite stopped loving him, you need further confirmation so that you can be able to move ahead with the recovery journey. Most often, we tend to rationalize things and fool ourselves that perhaps we need one more time to heal, while in reality, we're not even close to stopping loving them. At this point, you have to be honest and kind to yourself, and it is only then that you can realize where you really need to be.

The major signs that you are still in love with him include:

- **You constantly think about him:** No matter how long you have been apart, you can't help but think about him and all the good times you had with him. You ask yourself if you tried enough to reciprocate the good things he did to you. You keep wondering what he is up to, even if you know that this has nothing to do with you. Constant thoughts about him are an indication that you are not over him and he occupies a special part of your heart.

- **You don't find a man that measures up to him:** You meet new people, and they try to endear you, but in everything they do, you wish they would do it your ex's way. Rather than meeting other people and forgetting about him, these new guys that you meet make him think about your partner all the more. Your heart is closed to welcome new people, and your ex is the yardstick you use to measure everyone else. Although this is difficult when you really need to move on, it is an important aspect if you want to indulge in the recovery journey and get back your partner.

- **You can't let go of the relationship souvenirs:** You constantly look at the things that he gave you or the stuff that you collected together - the pictures, the gifts, and every other item - and you can't help but realize how wonderful your ex was. The kind of emotional attachment that comes with such mementos makes you realize that you still love him.

- **He is the first person you want to tell when something good happens to you:** You have to constantly fight the urge to reach him out and tell him what you achieved during the day. You want him to keep holding this role in your life, and you are longing for the connection that you had before things blew up. If this urge can't seem to go away after some time, it seems you still love him.

It's important that you learn to differentiate between loving him but not needing him and loving him and needing him altogether. The fact that you miss him and want to share everything that goes on in your life with him does not mean that he is the right partner for you. It will never make sense to put your ex before your happiness and get him back only for you to entangle yourself in a mixture of mostly bitter feelings.

The right partner is the one that you love and need. Below is a list of qualities in your previous relationship that point to a good partner for you:

- **You had a great relationship:** The reason you're remembering all the souvenirs is not because of what he used to lure him to idealize him during the honeymoon stage of the relationship, but because throughout the relationship, you had trust, respect, and open communication. You were each other's cheerleader; you tried working as a team, but maybe you both did not know how to accommodate each other's point of view. Now you know better, and you realize there are some great aspects that can help you build up your relationship again.

- **The breakup was circumstantial and a quick decision:** Most great relationships break because of quick decisions. Maybe you gave up too easily. Maybe you were too full of yourself at the time and were not ready to decrease your ego. Maybe you overreacted, or perhaps, maybe you broke up too soon after realizing that one of you was going to move to a distant location and you called it quits. In this case, given another chance, the relationship has the ability to work well for both of you.

- **Your friends and family find it a good idea for the two of you to get back together:** Most often we live in a cocoon of self-denial and tend to overlook things that our true friends and family point out. However, the truth is that these people can see beyond what we are able to see or admit when in a relationship. Therefore, listen to their sentiments of you getting back together. If they support the idea, you might want to try to get him back.

- **You see the potential in the relationship:** Anyone who thinks they're in love with their ex-partner will always be tempted to think that there is potential in the relationship. Most often, however, this is not the case. Such false hope may keep you holding on to someone who was and never will be worth your time. The only ex-partner that you need is the one who you love and need - the one who you objectively find potential in.

Are you ready to compromise?

Establishing that you still love and need your partner is one thing, but deciding if you are ready to give up some part of yourself is another. Remember, you are two people with different needs and values. In fact, your relationship may have ended because one of you felt ignored and misunderstood. Any healthy relationship requires a great deal of compromise. You have to be ready to accommodate your partner and reason with each other to meet on a middle ground. Remember, both men and women have different needs in a relationship. Also, remember that each of you has different ideas of what makes a relationship work. You can't expect compatibility and your relationship to work if you are not ready to compromise.

Compromise is the ultimate requisite for you and your partner to balance each other's needs and come to a mutual understanding. Even before you get your partner back, you should ensure that you are willing to compromise, which makes it more likely for him to compromise as well. A great relationship is founded on trust and commitment, because this encourages open and honest communication, especially whenever there is a disagreement. Do not try to always be the right person in every situation, and be sure to let your partner win in some fights. Choosing to not compromise will reduce your chances of keeping your man, no matter how much effort you use in attracting him back to you.

SECTION 2: STEP BY STEP PROGRAM TO RECOVERY

***

Chapter 4: Introduction to the Step by Step Program

The need for a systematic approach

It is a good practice to use a systematic approach to solving every issue in your life. A journey of a thousand miles begins with a single step, experts say. Yours may not be a thousand-mile journey, but it is still a journey. Though it can seem trivial, the task of getting your ex back and having a quality relationship is not as easy. You might be tempted to think that just because he loved you and probably misses you, it is easy for you to get him crawling back to you by trying some random approaches. However, remember that they also have a life and plans that are different from what you are planning; hence getting them to fall back for you may be quite a daunting task. Mistakes may occur, because at this time you are heartbroken, confused, and vulnerable. You may make decisions and take actions that you will regret for the rest of your life due to tarnishing the image your ex has of you. A systematic

29

approach gives you an easy and stress-free life, because you know what you are doing next and what you want to achieve in every step.

In life, there is always a great reward in approaching issues systematically to keep everything on track. Systems are the foundations of success, because they provide you with inner guidance to allow you the power of forming habits. To give yourself a boost after understanding everything that your self-assessment reveals, you need to develop an improvement plan and make the commitment to be consistent with your plan. Improvement does not happen overnight. In fact, experts say that a habit develops fully in a 6-week timeframe (Lally & Gardner, 2013). Therefore, do not get frustrated if you cannot see progress in what you will be trying to achieve. Only make consistent efforts and be ready to live the daily life of a person with a purpose. Be patient with yourself, and the results will reveal themselves eventually. Do not fear to be a work in progress, because life is a constant learning process. Whenever you learn something new, put it to use, and don't let it slip through your mind. Try to eliminate your bad daily habits such as procrastination, unhealthy feeding, and laziness. Even the most successful people have taken deliberate efforts to develop daily good habits that help them live a rewarding lifestyle.

Essentially, the four-week program provides you with a systematic approach to recovering your lost relationship. It guides you into letting things flow and not rushing into any decision or action. The program is based on a good understanding of your mission so that you can remain focused throughout the four weeks. It eliminates the urge to be subjective to your feelings, especially when triggered by something you did not expect from your ex. As you may be aware, not every reaction from him as you begin to attract him back may make you happy. In fact, he may do things to test your ability to relapse back to old habits of making decisions based on your feelings. Therefore, following this program reminds you of what you are focusing on. You have a series of steps to follow, and there are minimal chances of getting lost along the way. Also, following these steps let you know that chances of success are high if you are able to complete the plan; hence you remain motivated even when frustrations along the way seem to pull you down. Thus, rather than doing things randomly to attract your ex, this program gives you the easiest way to recover your relationship.

What the program entails

The program entails daily activities that you do every week. It also includes a goal for every week. Each week's goal brings you closer to getting your ex back, and being tactful in every step increases your chances of them considering to be in a relationship with you again.

In week 1, you will take the first step, which is hiding your insecurity and neediness from your partner. You are instructed on the importance of this goal and also given the daily activities you can undertake to achieve it.

The second week is when you are encouraged to become a better self. After learning how to minimize contact with your ex in week 1, you are now provided with the tactics of becoming the better version of yourself. Old is boring, especially when the old self has a lot of aspects that need improved upon. During this week, you will apply most of what your self-evaluation, (as explained in chapter 3) reveals about you.

During the third week, you will learn how to contact your ex and make him notice you in a constructive way. You are given the right daily habits pertaining to contacting your ex the right way and at the right time. This is a big step in your recovery journey, because how you reach out to them matters a lot. You will learn how to handle any kind of response that your ex gives you and what to do about it.

Week four is the final step of your great journey. You get to meet with your ex purposefully and identify the best time for you to meet. You learn about the dos and don'ts and how to dress, speak, and identify if you also like the new him that you just met. Remember, it is not only about presenting the better you to him, but it is also about getting to know if you really like who he has become and how he behaves when you meet.

This program teaches you to be open-minded about your situation, but it also guarantees you success if you are keen to follow it. You must set your mind to be ready to undertake every step along the way cautiously and to be patient until you have completed the four-step journey.

Chapter 5: Stop Appearing Needy and Insecure (Week 1)

This phase is all about eliminating the tendency of following your confused and vulnerable attitudes towards your partners. Getting needy, desperate, and insecure is a deadly mistake that you can make around your ex. Panicking and pleading may occur to you as the next rational thing to do.

The reason you want to get back with your ex may be because you are dependent on him, and you think that you can only feel safe, loved, and happy with them. Yes, it is a reflex reaction of the mind to experience this panic whenever you feel like your sense of security might not be returned. However, rather than making your ex come back for you, this feeling will have you being abusive, manipulative, a stalker, jealous, and even unnecessarily angry. These are not behaviors you want to portray to someone that you want back.

There is absolutely no shame in admitting to your insecurities and even low self-esteem. Furthermore, earlier chapters encouraged you to be honest with yourself for you to engage in a journey worth taking - that of recovering your ex. The problem only comes when you let these insecurities occupy the better part of your brain and influence your reasoning. It will make you do things that will not only shame you in front of your boyfriend but will leave you in a more hurtful position than you are right now.

It will translate that you seek the validation of your partner, and you will not be doing yourself justice. It will also show them that they have great control over you, yet every man wants a woman that can maintain good behavior even when they have unresolved issues. Also, it will show them that you are still nagging, yet this may have been the reason you broke up. Every man needs a woman who loves herself enough to know that there is a life to live beyond their relationship; one who does not put him in front of her needs. When you appear needy and insecure, it means that you demonstrate these behaviors because you are miserable without them. Maybe this distance between you two was a natural way of helping you realize that you don't need anyone to be happy or to be approved by anyone for your esteem levels to rise.

Therefore, it is recommended that you are as objective as you can be and that you make no decisions based on any odd thoughts or insecurities.

Week 1: Goals of the week

By the end of this week you will have learned:

- To stop appearing needy and insecure to your ex partner

- How to keep a safe distance

- How to handle the following 3 weeks of the recovery process

Minimal contact and keeping a safe distance

The basic rule of thumb you should hold in this phase is that you give your ex what they asked for: space. Whether or not you are the one who led to the breakup, your ex needed space. Maybe issues were unsolvable at the moment, and they were experiencing a change in their lives that they felt you would not be part of. Maybe they needed to give you some space to reorganize your thoughts and realize if you really wanted the relationship. In any case, space was necessary. Therefore, do not call them all the time; this is perhaps the greatest mistake you can make around your ex, which may lead to adverse reactions from him such as blocking you on all platforms, including calls, text messages, and even on social media. They could also begin to ignore your contact, and this will hurt you more.

In fact, did you know that the mere thought of contacting him even once is a mistake? It is good for you to know this. This is important, because you want him back and contacting once may be one of the biggest steps that lead to your success in having them back. You may imagine that maintaining frequent contact will prevent him from moving on or forgetting about you, but the truth is that you are fooling yourself. It portrays neediness and it is very unattractive.

In this phase, keep the communication minimal. Don't call, text, ask about them from friends, or even hang out in common places. This is your time to reorganize your thoughts and remove all the negativity that may have come from your breakup; give your ex some time alone, and also gather confidence before approaching him. When you finally reach out to them or meet with them, you want it to be worthwhile.

The following are some of the golden rules to remember:

- Do not inform your ex that you are not going to be talking to him unless he is calling you. You may answer the call and tell him that it is just not a good time for you to talk. Keep them guessing what is happening with you. Just avoid talking to him.

- Do not be afraid that this space might make your ex move on and forget about you. You need it for your mental wellness, and it is unlikely that he will meet someone and marry them instantly.

- If you led to the breakup, you might be tempted to think that, because you did not put much effort into the relationship, that this silence is not for you. However, keeping in touch frequently only shows them that you are just a needy woman with no regard for other people's feelings and values.

- If you live or work at the same place, not contacting each other is going to be tough. If it is possible for you to leave for the week, then this is recommended. If it is not possible, make sure there is minimal contact and only when it is really important that you talk - nothing personal.

Do not beg or try to use pity. Begging only makes you appear needy and as aforementioned, no man wants to be with a needy and insecure woman. Especially not today, when there are various confident women out there who understand how to relate with men.

You can rest assured that your ex will not take you back because of pity. Even if they did, you will be making a fool of yourself, because rather than commanding respect, you are pitied. You will start to be looked at as someone who can't stand on their own and whose survival depends on their man.

The best thing for you to do is to take time, be composed, gain confidence, and then approach him. Whenever thoughts that he will come back to you when he sees you miserable cross your mind, make sure your ex is not allowed to see you.

Do not bombard them with affection all the time. You may be tempted to think that just because you show your ex love and affection all the time, they want you back. This is not the case. You want to take this chance and reorganize your thoughts. Remember, your aim is to tactfully twist events and make him come back even if you were the cause of the breakup.

He already knows you love him out of the time that you stayed together. The differences that came in between your relationship did not really make you stop loving him. You do not need to dwell on the obvious, because repeating yourself and him responding by saying that he already knows is a clear sign that you are losing the battle. The more you shower him with love, the more suspicious he will be about your intentions, and the further away from you he will want to be.

Additionally, obsession is the worst feeling you can have at this moment. You are already trying to figure out if your ex misses you and if they would like to have you back as much as you do, but you cannot let these feelings define you. In fact, this is the phase when you should strive to drop all these misleading feelings and focus on your mission. This obsession over how you can get back together and the endless and useless questions that linger in your mind can be the greatest cause for your disappointment. Obsession is detrimental, because you try to figure out whatever is going through his mind, yet it is impossible to get the correct answers to these questions. You are simply going ahead of time and finding answers before you're even able to see each other. This is overworking your mind, and it can interfere greatly with your sound thought process.

Constructive attention seeking

Do not let them get away with everything. Instead, have a say in your interactions. Wanting to reconcile with your ex may make you forget that you have your own needs to be met in the relationship. This is especially the case if you are the one who caused the breakup. You have now realized that it was your mistake and you feel like your ex is justified for everything they say. This is not the case. Be wise, and be apologetic, but let them know that you can't take everything they say at face value.

Even if your ex ends up feeling entitled to make some demands in the first phase, do not accept everything. Just because you contacted them once and they responded swiftly, you should not go all out showing them that they can say anything and you will follow. This only reduces their sense of respect for you. Remember, your goals and your desires matter. Also, every man wants a woman who can challenge him positively, speak for herself, and remain respectable. Therefore, have your reservations when responding to anything they may say if they say anything at all.

It's important that you do not freak out if they have moved on into another relationship. Did you think that you were the only person that would make him feel satisfied? Did you think you were the first person your ex ever dated? Well, if he was able to move on from their ex and have a happy relationship with you, you can be sure that he can also move on.

The problem is most common when they seem like they have moved on very quickly. This might make you furious and lead you to imagine that maybe they left you for that other woman. You start getting jealous over the other woman, and this is a bad attitude when you are trying to recover your boyfriend. Sometimes you may even be tempted to stalk the other woman to identify how you can compete with her over your man. You may even find yourself bad mouthing this new person to your ex and telling him how wrong she is for him. If this is the attitude that you have, then your chances of winning back your man are minimal.

Also, being irrational may make you retract your efforts of getting him back, while he may be in a rebound relationship that will end in the near future. Most often, a rebound relationship shows that he was hurt by your breakup and just wants to be somewhere he is feeling appreciated for a moment to avoid grieving. It does not necessarily mean that he has forgotten about you and will not have you back if he still has a soft spot for you. Therefore, just be cool about it, and never think of mentioning the other woman while in this process of recovery. Instead, use your tactics to make him realize the value in you, and he will make a deliberate move to be with you.

It's also important that you don't call your ex names. Sometimes, due to anger caused by insecurities and a lack of emotional control, you may find yourself calling your ex names. Anger, resentment, and negative emotions are not a surprise at this moment. You are already irritable and sad that he is not by your side. On top of that, the man may provoke you. Everyone has some angry moments; the man might even be angry at you, perhaps for the behavior that led to your parting. Remember, this time is not about justifying your anger, but rather it's about remaining calm until you're able to talk on a one-on-one basis and soberly table your concerns.

Calling them names, saying sarcastic comments, or making fun of them is a sign of disrespect, and it is definitely not desirable. Every man wants to be respected by his woman. To avoid getting to this point, make sure that you are well composed whenever talking to him, and try to imagine all of his good attributes and how good your relationship was. This will allow you to avoid anger and think constructively.

Take care of how you use your social media profiles. After a breakup, most people are tempted to get back at each other through social networking sites. It is like some form of a competition whereby you post while striving to make each other see how horrible your partner was, how you are doing better without them in a bid to get them jealous, or how desperate you are without them. This is by no means a constructive way of seeking attention.

It is hard to disagree that social media has become a great enemy to relationships in various ways. One downfall of the internet is that it never forgets, and once you have posted something out there, it is with the public. The power of smartphones and screenshots keeps you grounded. You may think posting an emotional message on Twitter or Facebook is easily reversible, but the truth is that you can never undo a mess that you make online. Therefore, be keen on how you use social media during this part of the recovery process. Some of the major rules to remember are as follows:

- **Do not block or unfriend unreasonably:** Remember that this is a person that you want to get back to. If you had already unfriended or dramatically blocked him, then you can only hope that it never bruised his ego. If you are still friends, let it stay this way. The best thing you can do is limit seeing any of his posts or activities.

- **Do not rush into deleting pictures:** Deleting pictures is among the things that cause alarm on social media and gets people into your business. If you had pictures of your ex, you might think that deleting them shows him how unhappy you are. However, this creates an impression towards people and everyone knows you broke up, even if he may have wanted to keep it private.

- **Do not announce that you're single:** Do not rush into posting how single you are, perhaps trying to capture his or his friends' attention. You should ensure that your profile is in a condition where no one else knows whatever you are going through and the process you are undertaking.

- **Do not post revenge stuff:** While it is normal to have these feelings, avoid posting anything that shows how you are feeling, because you may start appearing needy, and this is one of the things you have to avoid to be successful in this process.

- **Do not stalk:** Unless you are doing your simple research trying to figure out how to contact your ex depending on the amount of time you've been apart, you should avoid following them and checking out their profiles and activities.

In fact, if you could keep off social media while going through this process, it is the best option. It will give you time to focus on yourself without the influence of all the social media folly. Remember, you are entering a period of self-improvement, and this requires some serious "you" time.

However, chances are that you have already made some of these mistakes when trying to contact your partner. Do not beat yourself up. Humans are meant to make mistakes, and our impacts make the world a beautiful place. It is now time to try to retrace your steps and ensure that you have understood all of this information before you move on to the next week.

Also, we have already established that the worst partner you can get back with is a narcissist; hence all these steps do not apply to getting back a narcissist. Know your limits, and eliminate contact with a narcissist fully. For any other reason that you may have broken up, including clashing values, a lack of communication, faded passion and affection, lack of support, or cheating, be sure to maintain minimal contact with your ex.

Overall, the ultimate goal for this week is to achieve a minimal contact period where you get to reorganize your thoughts and give your ex some space while ensuring that, when you are ready to contact them or see each other, it will be worthwhile.

Other constructive activities to do this week include:

- **Keeping off the phone if not in use:** One of the greatest temptations people have at this moment is their phone, especially when in leisure. You might be tempted to just send him a message and ask him how he is doing. Also, when you always have your phone, you may be tempted to talk to people about your plan, which may, in turn, get ruined in the process. People will always have ideas, and not all are necessary. You surely want to avoid this and focus. You are the only one who understands this process, and you do not need interference. Furthermore, staying off the phone prepares you to begin the following step of being productive with your life. You cannot expect to have good daily habits for improving yourself if you always have a phone with you. You have to admit that it is a great source of distraction.

- **Keeping off social media:** Social media is another potential source of distraction. You are human, and sometimes you may get carried away and begin getting into stalking mode. Remember that you are trying to avoid doing anything on social media that may make your partner lose further interest in you. Also, you may get distracted along the way. As such, you should avoid social media.

- **Talking to family and close friends about general stuff:** Since you need to ensure that at any given time your mind is sober, you need to have your support system close to you. You don't necessarily have to inform them of everything that you are doing, but you sure need someone to talk to. This will help keep your energy levels up and clear your mind of any dull moments.

- **Watch your favorite type of content and get entertained:** Besides talking to family and close friends, you should take some time away from any other noise and listen and watch stuff that calms your soul and raises your spirits. Do not entertain content that disturbs your mind, lest you lose your focus.

- **Maintain a journal:** As with any other important journey of your life, a journal should be your closest friend all throughout the process. The greatest value of a journal is that it offers you a chance to be honest with yourself and to enhance your retrospective skills. Through the journal, you can identify any of your triggers that might make you return to old habits. Be sure to write down anything that causes you to become emotional - either happy or sad - every day.

Week 1 resume: achievements, tip & advice

At the end of the week, be certain to set aside a good time to go through your journal, making sure that you can identify any of the weaknesses that you have noted in the past few days and how you plan to address them so that it does not interfere with your recovery process in the next steps that you are about to take.

How do you feel now? You have now come to the end of week 1, which has basically shown you how to be an independent lady and maintain objectivity in all your decisions involving your ex so that you don't appear needy and insecure. Remember that no matter how tough this week has been for you trying to keep a distance, you have made it. Therefore, you should be motivated to carry on with the rest of the journey. A step at a time is all it takes. You may be feeling confused and still anxious to know what he has been doing while you were silent or whether he will want to have you back, but you should stay as positive as possible and maintain your focus. You will grow stronger as the days go by, and by the end of the journey, you will be happy that you did not give up.

Do not forget to: Keep updating your journal so you can keep track of your moods, actions, and behaviors.

Advice of the week: You are not needy; you are learning to become independent, and you are preparing to improve yourself in the critical areas of your life. Do not forget that the end result should be to present yourself in a way that your ex boyfriend cannot resist but take you back.

Chapter 6: Strive to Become a Better Person (Week 2)

At this point, you should be striving to become a person who you can be proud of. Getting your ex-boyfriend back is the objective here, but remember that you need to be the best version of yourself first. It is good to go back to your ex as someone new or after having changed several things. You can call this adding value to yourself such that they won't only be interested in you, but it will be hard for him to resist you. You may think that concentrating only on getting your ex back and putting the other things on hold is the best option. This will be a mistake, because you will be going back to him the same way you left, and so he won't see any changes in your life. When engaging in a relationship, nobody is perfect, and what people often choose to do is make a compromise. In certain cases, depending on how the relationship ended, both you and your ex may have compromised on something that ended up beginning to be a bother. For instance, maybe you were a college dropout, and your boyfriend has no issue with this, but because there is poor communication subconsciously, he may have thought that the reason for the poor communication is because you did not finish college. This is an example that signifies the need to make improvements in your life.

Although this is a tremendous time for a person to make progress in life, it is also the part where most people make mistakes. This is a time when you have no contact with your ex; hence, it is an opportunity for you to make a positive change in your life. You should not just sit around, eat junk food, get into drinking, and be miserable for the next month or two waiting to contact him. Truthfully, things will not favor you, even after the no contact period. You need some time to grieve after the breakup, and it will be helpful to spend some time analyzing your relationship, grieving, and being alone. However, you need to balance that out with things that make you a better person and doing things that you enjoy. Although you want your ex back, learn what makes you happy without him. We will touch on some ways you can improve yourself in the remainder of the chapter.

Week 2: Goals of the week

At the end of the chapter, you will have learned how to do the following:

- Enhance your physical and mental capacity

- Drop negative habits and behaviors

- Improve your academic and professional achievement

Enhance your physical appearance and mental capacity

Truth be told, in most cases when a person has settled in the relationship, they are not keen on their appearance compared to how they looked when single. Now it is time for you to make a change in your physical appearance. Do not make it worse by letting yourself get carried away by stress, anxiety, or depression. Each of these cases will either make you lose weight significantly or make you become overweight. Most people fail in realizing the value there is in making a positive change in their appearance and not engaging in toxic activities. For instance, if you start drinking heavily or using hard drugs now that you are grieving, you will be making many steps backward. You do not want this to be the case if you wish to get your ex back.

Next time your ex sees you, he should see a new you in a positive way. There are simple things you can do such as get a new haircut or hairstyle. It is a simple act but with a tremendous effect on you. When you look at the mirror, you will begin to see someone new. Another thing you can do is get your teeth cleaned, which is something you may have not thought about or thought was adequate to do on your own. Go to an expert, and by the end of your visit, you will have a very attractive smile. Similarly, go to a doctor to receive a thorough medical check-up. Do not underestimate the value of small things like having your blood pressure, sugar level, body mass ratio, and weight checked; it's also important to see if you have any sexually transmitted diseases. Always remember that you are doing this for yourself to perfect yourself, not necessarily for your ex-boyfriend alone.

The other change you need to make is to get the best body shape you possibly can. You may have never gone to the gym, or perhaps it has been years since you went there. Now it is time to get back there. Start small until your body becomes used to being exercised. A morning run is also beneficial if you're unable to go to the gym. Working out is great for your mental health, because it can boost your endorphins and make you happy. It is one of the most credible ways to escape bad or evil thoughts. Most people uncover their body shape after exercising and working out. This is your opportunity to put in hard work to get that desirable body, and the only way you will do that is by stepping out of your comfort zone. You may have heard that working out improves self-esteem and discipline. By working out, you can attain the body that you had when you met your ex, or you can attain a shape that he has never seen on you. You should also think about buying new clothes. This will help you achieve a new look and make you feel better.

Enhance your mental capacity

Breaking up with someone is overwhelming. As noted, most people fail to realize that they can use this period to their benefit. You ought to note that when getting back with your ex, being a happy and confident person is vital. The only way that you can realize confidence and happiness is by working on yourself. The following are some of the ideas that can assist you in avoiding stress, anxiety, and depression.

- **Take time to grieve:** People react differently to stressors. You may be the kind of person who likes to grieve to the point that they are significantly carried away or lose themselves. Also, you may be the kind of person that tends to be in denial, and you will act strong even when hurting; it is only later that the reality of the situation will hit you. It is recommended that you give yourself some time to grieve. It will be difficult to move on if you do not put the breakup behind you. It is hard to be jovial after a breakup, so you should give yourself some time every day to grieve. It is okay to not eat properly, not sleep well, or to think about your ex every day, as it is part of the healing process to feel sorry and sad, but you have to do something to make yourself feel good.

- **Write a journal:** This is one of the oldest techniques and remains to be therapeutic. You will be writing about your thoughts and your emotions. As mentioned earlier, a journal will help you be more honest with yourself. It will definitely help in releasing all the emotions that would have been building up inside. In most cases, stress and anxiety may turn into depression, but through writing, you will be able to release it. More so, you will be able to look back and appreciate your journey of improvement every time.

- **Hang out with friends:** At this time, it is good to avoid being alone for long. Although it is good to grieve, ensure that you have time for friends and families. Your loved ones are people who will be there for you no matter what you are going through. By engaging with them, you may even realize that they have gone through the same situations or even worse ones. It is important to have a good time with them because it provides you with more perspectives on life.

- **Do some yoga and meditation:** Yoga and meditation are some of the suitable ways a person can improve their physical and mental wellness. These activities are great for realizing self-awareness. Although it sounds obvious, self-awareness is not as easy to achieve as some may think. Most people do not take time to really uncover their strengths and weaknesses. Nobody is perfect, and what a person can do is build on their weaknesses and try to turn them into strengths. Meditation will pave the way for you to understand yourself so you can then accept who you are. It is something that builds up confidence in life.

- **Go out on a date:** Do not be surprised that something like this is being recommended. You cannot be certain about whether your ex is truly the one unless you have another perspective about the relationship. You can even go out on a few dates see what you find out there, listen to how you feel, and be sure of what you want. The only way that you get new perspectives on life is by meeting new people.

Dropping negative habits and behaviors

In most cases, you may find that it is your behavior or habits that led to the breakup. It is your time to write any wrongs and be someone better by upholding proper morals and principles. You have to address all these issues, working on them to make a positive change to ensure that when you get him back, none of this will cause a problem in the relationship.

- **Cheating:** If you are the one who cheated, you have to honestly address this issue. Ask yourself what made you cheat. Do you think that you could have avoided this? Do you think you will repeat this act? Most people in a relationship find out that they have cheated either because they were having a conflict with their partners or because they were drunk and vulnerable. If it is your partner who cheated, ask yourself what role you could have played in this. As noted, things such as insecurity can drive your partner away and may make them cheat. In any way that it may have happened, you need to be honest with yourself and focus on rectifying your contribution to it. You do not have to beat yourself up or blame yourself at this point; what you are doing now is making a promise that you won't do this again.

- **Being unsupportive:** Being supportive is a very important thing in a relationship that can help make your partner feel appreciated, loved, and connected to you. The term "power couple" implies people who support each other in their endeavors. Especially at a young age, one is trying to figure out what to do, and they look to others regarding what to build in their life. Your boyfriend may have given you enough opportunities, hoping that you will become supportive, until they realize that you were never going to change. Now it is time to stop being selfish and look forward to helping them achieve their goals. You will begin to be supportive of those who are close to you, such as family members and friends, where you give them ideas on what they have to do. Also, learn about encouraging, motivating, and delivering moral support to others.

- **Inability to commit or lack of trust:** Most people fail to commit to a relationship because of trust issues. There are other reasons, as well, and whatever they are, they may have pushed your ex away. When facing these issues, ask yourself why you did not want to commit or rather why it is hard for you to trust someone. When you begin with this, it will be easy for you to start making positive strides toward rectifying this issue. There is no need to try to get your ex-boyfriend back if you know that you will not be able to commit to them - if that is what they want.

- **Improve your communication skills:** Proper communication skills is a challenge for many people. They fail to find the right words or approach to use with a person when there is a dispute. Learning how to communicate begins with listening to others. Let people tell you their side of the story, and then from there, you will be able to debate or negotiate. Also, if a person has done something wrong to you, politely ask them the reason why they acted in that manner. In this case, you have to ask yourself whether you have the tendency of jumping to conclusions. You can search for proper communication skills on the internet, but practically engaging it is vital.

- **Learn to show passion and affection:** It is a negative thing when you are in a relationship with someone yet you are not able to show them affection and passion. This is much simpler to fix than you might think; it only requires the use of positive and lovely words. Also, using simple acts like holding hands, cuddling, and even leaning on your boyfriend is important. A person knows that he or she is loved by being shown affection and passion. Since you know you failed to show it, be ready to manifest it if you get back together.

There are numerous behaviors and habits that may have pushed your ex to the point of breakup. When it comes to relationships, there tend to be similar things that cause issues. The point herein is that, while making improvements, it is important that you address these issues properly. Whether you will need to seek guidance and counseling or read about them, it is important that these behaviors come to an end. Besides those discussed above, you may need to deal with your controlling nature, extreme jealousy, insecurity, lack of personal hygiene, or lack of social skills.

Enhance your academic or professional achievements

When striving to be a person who you are proud of being, you should not forget about academic and professional achievements. If circumstances allow you to get more education, you should go for it. If you did not finish your college education, enroll and finish it. Maybe you have always wanted to get a second degree or masters; this is your chance to do so. There are certain cases where a person puts their dreams and goals at a standstill. This is the time to revive those goals and dreams, especially if it related to academic and professional achievement. The reason for this section is to improve you in all ways. There is nothing more disturbing than dreams or goals that you know you could have achieved but you deliberately failed to do so. Although you and your partner may have settled on the level of education that you have already received, it is important to make some improvement to this.

Education is tied to the ability to improve a person's integrity and their understanding of the things around them. It provides exposure to things in life that you may not have encountered before. Especially when it comes to the classroom environment, it is a suitable area to know the emerging issues even unlike the workplace environment. You may enroll for a three-month course, such as one related to project management, advanced computer skills, accounting, entrepreneurship, human relations, psychology, cooking, or anything you ever wanted to learn about. If you can't think of any interests regarding what to learn, search for something that you may like to know more about, such as music, drawing, painting, or simple construction techniques. You will be surprised how you can be changed by the end of the course. It is a venue to gain a new perspective, not only about life but also about people. Know that you are doing these things for yourself and for your own good, and the unseen benefits will surprise you. You may come to realize that engaging with other people has enhanced your communication, self-esteem, and social skills, among others.

Professional achievements will take different forms depending on the position you are in currently. For instance, let's say you were not working or you just had a simple job, yet you are qualified for something bigger. Now it is time to look for your dream job, apply for opportunities, and pursue any possible avenues that could help you to find this job. Or perhaps you are working one job, yet you have extra time for a part-time job. You need to go ahead and look for this job, as it will help to improve your financial status, skills, and exposure. You will be proud of yourself if at this point you have become a hard-working person. There is no need wasting time when, by doing extra work, you can get your dream car, your dream house, and financial independence. By the end, you will be proud of yourself and proud of what you have achieved.

Also, you may have a good job but you just do ordinary things. You are in the comfort zone; you need to move out of it to realize your full potential for personal satisfaction. Set personal goals and objectives at your work, and look forward to achieving them. You have to challenge yourself, and if you find yourself needing to get more training, it is important that you do so. Surprise yourself by going for the promotion that you wanted or thought was out of your reach. It all lies in performing better and exceedingly compared to the others.

If you pay attention to yourself and focus on becoming the best version that you can be, you will be surprised. It is true that in most cases people tend to settle with what they have achieved, not because they cannot achieve more, but because they want to stay in their comfort zone as Lefebvre, H. (2017) suggests. The truth is, if you want things to resonate with you, then you have to engage and start working on them. Try out all possible ways to realize your full potential, even if it entails speaking to a counselor or a life coach. At the end of it all, make sure you are becoming someone your ex will not be able to resist.

Week 2 resume: achievements, tip & advice

Now that you have come at the end of this week synthesize the following questions.

How do you feel now? At this point you have followed the proper steps that enable you to achieve the best version of yourself. You feel proud to have achieved the body shape you have always desired. You have attained proper mental capacity, making you an objective person. Also, you have dropped undesirable behaviors and enhanced your academic and professional achievement. At the end, you now feel self-confident and have high self esteem.

Do not forget to: Update your journal and make self improvement and enhancement activities your norm.

Advice of the week: Engage in the noted activities willingly and with dedication, knowing that it is all for your wellbeing. It is vital for self-awareness and self realization as this will include benefits beyond getting your ex back.

Chapter 7: How to Finally Contact your Ex (Week 3)

You have come far to get to this point. If you have adequately followed the steps that have been noted thus far and modified them in a manner so that they would help to improve you further, then this is a tremendous success. You have most likely surprised yourself and the people around you due to what you have achieved. You may not have thought that you could achieve this, and if you did, then you were not confident enough.

☆ *If you have gotten this far and have achieved more than you thought possible, please consider leaving a short review for the book on Amazon, it means a lot to me! Thank you.*

There are only a few relationships that end in a way that the partners have arrived at a good agreement. In most cases, people are angry and feel confused with one another. At this time, it is not surprising to realize that they thought you were desperate, clingy, and needy person. It is not surprising for someone to make you out to be a person with little self-respect.

Now that you have not been in contact with them and you are doing fine on your own, they must be wondering what happened to you. At this point, they no longer look at you as the desperate person they thought you were. It is natural that how they think about you now includes the positive aspects that they used to associate with you - what was it that they were attracted to when you first met? This is the perfect time for you to talk to them, perhaps even face-to-face. It will be a surprise to see the new and improved you, a version of you they may have never imagined. Maybe they expected that you are somewhat depressed and trying to get over them without having a positive focus on your life. They will be asking themselves what could have brought this positive change in you.

You should know that to be in this position requires you to do several things. One thing you need is determination because, without it, you will not make even the first step. No matter how difficult and overwhelming it is, you should always be focused. Then you need to actually bring positive change in your life. However, this is still not enough; you need to become an attractive, happy, and confident person. After this, it is time for you to contact your ex and meet with him somewhere.

Week 3: Goals of the week

At the end of this week, you will have learned:

- The appropriate time to contact your ex

- The right approach to adopt in contacting your ex

- When and how to ask your ex out

The right time for contacting your ex

You may now be wondering when the right time to contact your ex is. The best answer to this question is when you are ready. Try not to feel rushed because, by the deadline you might set, you may not be ready emotionally, physically, and mentally. You have to ensure that the new you is the person making the contact now. Do not focus on making contact with your ex because you are estimating that by that time, they already miss you very much. Remember that it is not about them but about you. The reason for this is because you have to be ready to handle to contact your ex in a mature manner. As your new self, you have to be rational and make this contact with an open mind. Be sure that you will be able to handle how they respond to you, and you won't appear desperate or needy again.

The issue of confidence was elaborated earlier in the book, as you may recall. It was emphasized that you should try to focus on building your behavior and habits and be confident with yourself. Confidence will be demonstrated by the way you act and how you talk. You should know that most women make mistakes by rushing to make contact with their ex-boyfriend when they are not actually ready. The reason for this is they think three months of being broken up is a long time, and they start to think that their boyfriends miss them already. There is no perfect time to make contact; if it takes you a year to reach this step, then you should adhere to this. You have to remember how men perceive relationships, emotions, and sex. If you have stayed for quite some time without seeing each other, they will be quick to say they miss you. Then you will most likely get intimate, and in no time, you may go back to being cold toward each other because they realize you are being less than genuine. It is due to this reason that you should have fully built up your self-confidence prior to contacting him.

Therefore, before you do make contact, be sure that you keep a few things in mind. Be certain that you followed the no contact rule clearly; this means that there were no text messages, phone calls, visits, Facebook messages, or contact through mutual friends. Also, it means that you are not checking out their status on Facebook or any other social media and commenting. Do not accidentally bump into him, because in doing so, you are clearly tampering with the process. The reason as to why the no contact rule is important is because it will help you to deal with addiction. You have to learn to live without them for you to stop being desperate or needy.

Also, ensure that you are not in the same status as you were directly after the breakup. In other words, be certain that you are not addicted, angry, needy, or in a situation where you may beg your ex to take you back. If you feel the same way and like nothing has changed then you are not ready. Also, ensure that you have made a few positive changes in your life. The implication in this is that you are now physically and mentally fit. Also, you have added value in yourself by taking a short course or anything that has made a positive impact in your life. If you are certain about this, then proceed to the next step. This step inquires as to whether you are unquestionably sure that getting back with your ex-boyfriend is a good decision and the right thing for you to do. It mostly depends on what you found out about them. Remember that realizing your ex is dating someone else immediately after breaking up with you should not be a major issue, because this may be a rebound relationship. Be sure to have clarified with your heart and mind that you want to have them back.

Moreover, check whether you went on at least one date during the no-contact period. The reason for going on a date is to have a new perspective, not only of life but also about your relationship. After going on a date, you may be surprised to learn that you had limited yourself. You may even come across someone who interests you more, but the importance lies in making sure that you gained another perspective. The next question that you need to ask yourself is whether you have accepted the breakup. After that, then you have to ask yourself whether you are okay with the fact that you may never get your ex back. As bad as it sounds, it might not work out for you for reasons such as your ex doesn't want you back or they found someone else; it's even possible that an ex-girlfriend of theirs came back to them after you and he broke up. This is why it is important that you have taken the time to make changes in your life, because this time you are ready.

Finally, you have to answer the question of whether you have accepted that even if you do not get your ex back, you will be okay, because there are numerous opportunities for you to find happiness and love. The fact that you managed to avoid contacting your ex for up to 60 or 90 days means that you survived the hardest part. Ensure that you have the right attitude for this or any outcome. Now that you have gone through all of the above checklists, then you can go ahead and contact him.

The right way to contact your ex

Today, there are numerous ways to contact someone because of advanced digital technology. Most people are on more than three social network platforms, with the leading ones being Facebook, Twitter, and Instagram. You are probably thinking about which of the numerous methods will you use to contact him. After no contact, the best way to get in touch with your ex is using a handwritten letter, an email, or a text. Do not be surprised that a handwritten letter is being recommended at this time and era. It is a unique take in this age of digital technology. However, instead of going through all the trouble, you may just want to use email or send them a text.

Do not dwell too much on the medium that you use in contacting your ex. What matters most is the content of the message you need to pass along. You should consider preparing a message that serves the three purposes outlined below.

The first purpose is to let your ex know that you have accepted the breakup. You should let them know that you understand that it is for the best the breakup happened. You need to counter the image that they may have in their minds of someone who is desperate and needy who is refusing to break up.

The second purpose is for you to apologize for anything that may have happened after the breakup. Try to create the sense that you have forgiven and forgotten everything in the past.

Finally, you want to inform them about something good that is happening in your life. You do not need to write pages about it, but you can just mention something that has happened in passing. The main reason for this is to leave them in suspense about what is happening in your life or rather to show them that there are good things going on in your life besides their absence. By just mentioning this, you have given them something to chew on; you have sparked their curiosity. If they wish to know what is happening in your life, they will text or call you to talk about it. At any given time, there are things happening in your life; in this case, the focus was on creating positive change in your life. The reason for emphasizing making positive change is so that when it comes to talking about your relationship, you will be talking about positive change.

If you sent a handwritten letter, you can follow up with a text message. If you did not send a text message, it is still a good and credible medium, but it will depend on how your ex-boyfriend is, so make a decision depending on this. You may ask why uses a letter or email. The advantage with either of this is they signify a change from how your ex sees or thinks about you.

The advantage of using text messages is that they build attraction with your ex. They have the qualities of being personal and short, and your ex will have to read them. A correctly designed text message will condition your ex to feel excited when they see your text. Text messages were discovered as a way of people having fun. What you need to ensure is that your text does not make you seem needy or desperate. It is recommended that you use some rules when sending a text to your ex.

You should never send an empty message to your ex; this would be a message that does not create a conversation or one that does not say anything. Refrain from sending texts such as, "I miss you", "Hey", or "How are you?" You should never express your feelings in a desperate way or even talk about getting together.

You should not argue with him or say something negative over a text. For instance, you should refrain from challenging or blaming him for not putting a little more effort into the relationship.

Instead, you can mention something that happened in your life that reminded you of them, for instance, such as a comedy, another movie, or even a song. Also, remind them of the good times that you shared together. It could be swimming, a dinner you went to a nice restaurant, or adventurous vacations you had together. Most importantly, inform them that you are happy and having fun by meeting new people in life. While there are numerous things you can include in text messages, just ensure that they are fun, positive, and subtle.

The essence of doing this and engaging your ex in texting is to eliminate the awkwardness that was there after breaking up. This is meant to turn him into a text buddy. You should move things slowly as you try to rebuild a connection and attraction through text messages before it comes to meeting face to face. You should only ask them out after you have texted enough and you also feel attracted to them.

Asking your ex out

Remember that you are on a mission to get your ex back. You think he is the one despite the reasons for the breakup. While you may have addressed the reasons for the breakup, and in your case, became conversational with them, this is not the case for your ex. Remember that if you are the one who wronged them, you have to prove that you are a new person who would not do the same things. Also, if you are the one who wronged them, then they want to know that you can forgive them. Although you have been texting, things are yet not well settled from where you left them. Sometimes your ex may be willing to text with you in a good manner, but they are not yet ready to meet with you face to face. Maybe they are sorry for what they did or they do not feel ready to get back

Keeping this in mind, the best course of action then is to avoid calling this a date at all costs. Do not get surprised when you say that it is a date and your partner gets defensive. The reason why you are not supposed to call it a date is to avoid the thoughts that you want to get back with them. Although you know you want to get back with him, there are still things that are yet to be clarified. What you want to do now is to go out with a friend, and then from there, you will build up an attraction. If you have followed the guidance of this book, then you will have two advantages when you meet - one is attractiveness and the other is confidence.

It is easy to get your ex to go out with you, because at one time in their life, they were attracted to you. Also, the two of you are not strangers; in fact, you are extremely familiar with one another. The best way to ask your ex-boyfriend to go out with you is by giving them a call. In certain cases, they may need you to engage in a slight push. Do this in a simple way. For example, you may tell them that you'd just like to meet for coffee, and it is no big deal. However, you should not push too hard. For instance, telling your ex that he broke up with you and broke your heart, and so he should do this for you is less likely to get them onboard.

Although it has come to this point, one thing you should be aware of is that your ex does not owe you anything. As such, you have to treat them similarly to the way you would treat someone you wish to get close with. When they agree to meet you, it means that there is a good chance that they might want to get back with you.

Week 3 resume: achievements, tip & advice

This has been a crucial week in the process of getting your ex back. The process seems promising and it seems possible for you dreams to come true. It is important that you note the following:

How do you feel now? You are happy and hopeful, noting that to this point, you have made tremendous progress. This is a major achievement in life whereby as an individual, you have approached your ex as a totally different person. You are not needy and proud of the current self. You will be able to face your ex without showing emotional weaknesses.

Do not forget to: Be objective about this program. Also, ensure that you are ready for this crucial stage, which is to finally contact your ex.

Advice of the week: It is important that you ensure that you have actually achieved self-confidence and self-esteem. Also, when engaging in conversation, do not appear needy or insecure. Remember the structure of the messages or texts, because this is important for creating an image of your new personality; you are a changed person and not the individual that your ex broke up with.

Chapter 8: How to Purposefully Meet up with Your Ex (Week 4)

Now it is time to meet up with your ex. In the back of your mind, you know that you want him back. It has likely been weeks or even months since you met, so meeting up with him will be overwhelming and exciting at the same time. You may be tempted to overstep and say it's all about how you have missed him and how you want him back, among other sweet words you may think of. Also, you may want to be all over him, touching and kissing him or rather to be affectionate. It is a bad idea to do this, as it may destroy all of the hard work it took you to get to this point. The advantage that you have herein is having managed to obtain happiness and confidence on your own. You must keep in your mind that there are two things you need to achieve before telling your ex what you really want, and this includes building trust and a connection with your ex.

You are the one who planned this from the beginning and knew exactly what your end game was. It means that when you meet up with your ex, they might be skeptical or confused. For instance, let's assume that the reason you broke up is that he cheated. If this is the case, then he will be wondering what you would want with him. Another example is that you were the one who was unsupportive and lacked commitment, yet now you want to meet. They cannot help but wonder what you really want. At the back of their minds, they will have questions related to whether you realized they love or you are in love with them. The essence of these aspects as mentioned here is to caution you against making any drastic moves before your partner gets completely comfortable with you.

Know that, although you have been texting for a while and have managed to build a certain degree of connection and attraction, they are wondering what is up with you. They cannot help but think you must have seriously changed or that it is a pretense. In their minds, they are debating whether you are desperate and needy. Since they do not really know your character at the moment, they may even say things just to test your reaction. So, it is important to be cautious and respond in an ideal manner.

Week 4: Goals of the week

The key goals in this chapter and final week is to engage in a productive meeting with your ex. You will learn about the following things:

- What to do and what not to do

- Figuring out the chances of getting back with your ex

The dos and don'ts

Do your homework and be ready for anything

The truth of life is that relationships are not permanent. This is probably not what you want to hear, but unfortunately, it is the truth. Since the time you broke up, there were two possible outcomes, one being that the breakup would make you strong and the other being you would never get together again. You should have been prepared to lose them when you met them. The fact that you are feeling that he is the one does not mean that they feel the same about you. The advantage that you have at this point is that you have managed to build self-confidence over time. Allow your mind to think of the different scenarios that meeting him can result in. The reason why it is emphasized that you do not make a move unless you are sure that you are ready is that if you are still feeling desperation and neediness, they will be able to sense this from afar. If this is the case, then you hardly have a chance of getting them back forever. It is more ideal to postpone or cancel your meeting if you think that you are still needy.

There are various ways to test whether you are ready, but the most suitable way is thinking about yourself in a bad scenario. Imagine you are sitting somewhere with your ex laughing and conversing about different things. Suddenly, he tells you that he met someone weeks ago that he thinks is amazing, and they have an intense connection. The question you want to ask yourself is how it makes you feel. The first thing you might feel is disappointment or sadness, which is normal. The real issue here is how disappointed you will be. Will you suddenly become depressed or even start crying? If the thought of your ex dating someone else makes you feel enormously sad, then you are not ready. However, if you experience normal disappointment or sadness, then it means that you are ready to meet with him.

How you behave during the meeting carries a lot of weight in this entire process. Just like you would have a certain kind of behavior in an interview, you also have to mind your behavior when you meet with your ex. Your verbal and non-verbal cues must be in sync, so you won't be saying one thing while your eyes are saying another thing. Avoid funny behaviors such as flipping your hair, biting your nails, or fidgeting around. Although you don't have to be formal, you need to ensure that he is interested in listening to you.

Watch out for post-breakup pretense tests

Remember the reasons why you broke up with your ex? Those reasons are still viable throughout the whole process of trying to get your ex back. Be ready for your ex to do or say things intentionally to determine whether you are still desperate or needy. They need to be sure that you have actually changed in the way that you have been trying to portray. Let's assume, for instance, that you were unsupportive during the relationship. They may mention something they are doing to see whether you will inquire about it or offer an idea or to see if you will dismiss this information. If you show no concern, then they will know that you haven't changed.

The best way to test you is to bring up something about the past intentionally to push your buttons. You may have been controlling or jealous during the relationship and they may mention something to see how you will react. If you are still jealous, your body language will give you away. The best way to deal with such a situation is to remain calm no matter what they say or do. Do not act desperate or angry, because when you do so, they will think that you are still your old self, and they will not want to take you back.

The best way to handle this challenge is to improve your communication skills. It is one of the areas of personal improvement that will greatly help you in this case.

Do not talk about getting back together

Remember the section of the book about being attractive, happy, and irresistible? The essence of being such is to usher your ex to begin chasing you. You know you want to get back with your ex, but let them believe that it's their idea. This is the first date or outing with him since the breakup, so it will not be convenient for you to suggest getting back together. For the first date, just focus on having a good time with them.

In the course of the conversation, the topic of getting together may come up. What you should do is talk less about this and listen more to what they say. He may even ask you what you think, which is a tricky question at this point. The most suitable response to give him would be that you still have feelings, but you have not thought about getting back together. Give an answer that implies that you are not sure that getting back together.

You may have thought this is the best opportunity. You may even be happy about it and want to jump at the chance for you to get back together, but do not be tempted. Remember that he broke your heart, or rather think of it as him possibly testing you. Also, if you are the one who broke his heart, the question you should ask yourself is whether you have changed or if you are a better person now. It is still early, and there are numerous questions that you have not gotten answers to yet.

Balance the relationship

Now that you are talking with your ex, you may be tempted to express your feelings to him. You should not do this, but instead, pay attention to the pace at which your ex is taking you within the relationship. You need to ensure that you have an equal relationship with them. Failure to balance the relationship will make your ex think that you are chasing after him. The implication in this is that you should check up on them in the same manner they are. Also, let them try to meet you in the same way that you want to meet up with them.

Being skeptical is important as you have been cautioned in the previous cases. You have to figure out how things are going with him before getting back together. It is through this observation that you will realize whether he is interested in making the relationship work or not. If he is not, then you are better off without him. Do not beat yourself up, because you gave it your best and showed them the best version of you.

Set boundaries

Besides the idea of your ex turning you down, the other thing that most people fear is being kept in the friend zone. It is not a good feeling to be put in the friend zone, yet you wanted to have them for yourself. When you are a friend, there are chances that they will be telling you who they are now dating and how it is going unless you won't entertain that conversation. Thus, to avoid this, the best thing to do is to set boundaries of what you are talking about and doing. Also, maintaining an equal relationship is tremendously helpful in this case.

It is possible for you to flirt with each other, but you should remain respectful. Therefore, try to refrain from sleeping with each other. Additionally, you need to be casual while also having sexual chemistry. Be his lover, but also remember that you are his ex-lover.

The fact that you are an ex-lover and want to get back with him means that he should not ask advice about someone he is dating. You need to make clear to them that you cannot talk about someone they are having sex with or dating. Be ready to walk away if they do not respect the boundaries. It is not the time to act desperate or needy - walk away. In doing so, they will respect you and eventually ask for your forgiveness.

Be reasonable about where you meet

As part of your homework, be sure that your ex is comfortable with the venue that you choose to meet at. Remember that, at this moment, you are still focused on capturing his attention. Although it should not be a place that you struggle to get to, it should be one that your ex would love. Be sure to keep it simple, and avoid suggesting the most luxurious place in town that you can think of. Also, when you are at your meeting place, such as a restaurant (which is a recommended location), do not look for the most costly item on the menu in a bid to show that you have raised your standards. Ask for a simple drink, but if you are hungry, do not be afraid to eat. Only be keen on what you ask for, since he is most likely the one who will pay the bill. Being reasonable with what you order from the menu is a good way to show your decency.

Choose your clothing wisely

Most of us think that perhaps interviews are the only meetings where you dress to impress. For this meeting with your ex, your outfit is as important as what you say. Apparently, your ex wants to see if your heart has become more admirable and if you have matured emotionally. However, remember that men are naturally visual beings. One thing you want to show is that you have improved your wardrobe, but you also want to avoid being too revealing. You don't want your chest or thighs out to keep him glued on you, because you are looking for a genuine connection. At the same time, you are trying to show him that you are smart physically and mentally. It's suggested that you be a very decent and smartly dressed woman on that day.

Be sure to carry all the necessary things that every lady should have with you. This can include a hand moisturizer should you go wash your hands, an umbrella should it rain or get too sunny while with him, and even a notebook and a pen.

Keep in mind that you have been maintaining a journal all throughout your journey. You have gotten used to noting things down, and you surely want to be impressive. Should a chance present itself that your ex wants to illustrate something, then you should be able to give him a book and a pen, all this time ensuring to remain calm and not make it appear to be a big deal.

Figure out your chances of getting them back

You are probably asking yourself how you'll know the chances you have of getting your ex back. Due to what happened, you want to be sure that you are both on the same page or rather that you want the same thing. Furthermore, you do not want to overstep your boundaries or ruin it by rushing or making a wrong assessment. There are numerous things to consider when looking at this. Remember that you have been working and preparing for this for quite some time. You are ahead of your ex, and perhaps they did not even think about getting back with you. It is after contacting them that you have ignited their interest in you, so they too may have started to want you back. However, they need to be sure that they are making the right decision. Thus, they may take some time before even suggesting that you get back together. Thus, you need to be considerate and aware of such a possibility.

During the day that you are meeting, ensure that you avoid anything that might trigger your mood. You have worked very hard to get this far in being your best self, but you could destroy this just by having your mood change moments before you meet up. Relax and get ready to meet him, keeping an open mind to accept any result. After all, you will have made yourself proud and will not go away blaming the results on something like how tense you were or how childishly you behaved.

Throughout the conversation, you will hold yourself together and be a good listener. Observe his verbal and non-verbal cues as he does yours. Notice everything, because this will help you figure out if you like the new him or if you would ideally have him change a few things. Listening skills are among the best attributes you can have in any form of communication. In fact, wise people usually listen more than they speak. While it is mostly upon you to spark a conversation, you don't have to be the one speaking all the time. Be patient with him, even if it takes quite a while for him to think of the words he needs to reply to you. You should also try your best to be strategic. You have probably predetermined a conversation in your mind, planning the right questions and comments to say to him one after the other. However, sticking to such a conversation may reduce your ability to listen to what he actually has to say. Instead of responding to a question that he asks you, you might be saying totally different things. Also, you will not be able to realize if you actually still want to be with him or not.

Since you don't want to make a quick decision as to whether he is worth getting back with, one of the best ways you can realize if the meeting is worth it and that your efforts are paying off is through the rapport that you two establish. Although there was a good reason that led to the breakup, your ex should be able to establish a reasonable degree of rapport with you. For instance, maintaining eye contact shows you that he is interested in what you have to say, and it is a way of increasing mutual attraction. Also, if he does not put barriers between both of you, it shows that he is welcoming. Barriers could include newspapers or a glass, or concentrating too much on the meal or drink that you are sharing. Wherever there is rapport, people try to eliminate any kind of barriers that may exist between them. Most importantly, you should establish the message that he wants to put across. One of the things you should watch out for is excessive pride and bragging. There is a fine line between testing your reaction and actually bragging about where he is at in life now. Also, his words should not degrade you or compare you to another person. These are signs of trouble, even if you get back together.

With that said, congratulations if through meeting there are signs of mutual interest in meeting up another time. You have managed to capture his attention in this case, and he would like to see you once again, or he has asked if he could have another chance with you. You have simply presented a version of yourself that he could not resist. As explained, you should not ask directly if you are getting back together. However, at this point, you have led him to ask the most awaited question or take the most preferred turn.

Week 4 resume: achievements, tip & advice

You have come very far to reach this point. It has been a success, and all the credit goes to you. Thus, we can affirm the following concerns:

How do you feel now? You are proud of yourself and what you have achieved, and most importantly, you are with the love of your life.

Do not forget to: note the progress in your journals. Also, ensure that you follow the dos and don'ts, and let it come from your heart.

Advice of the week: Do not fake, but rather, be your new self - someone who knows what is good for them and how to treat other people well. Let your ex know that the changes are deeply rooted in you. Remember the test questions, and do not be quick to show your emotions, as this will make you appear needy. Calmness is an important tool and a secret weapon, so use it well.

SECTION 3: KEEP THE FIRE BURNING AFTER GETTING YOUR EX BACK

***

Chapter 9: How to Avoid Losing Him Again

By now you know the fate of your mission. You have either succeeded or failed. If you have failed, maybe you took some incorrect steps. However, the chances are high that you have your man back. Now it is time to build a great relationship and ensure that he never leaves you.

Factors that make a relationship last

It might seem trivial, but understanding some of the core pillars of a healthy and long-lasting relationship may help save your relationship. Having already experienced what it feels like to be apart from the person that you love and realizing that there is a great potential for the relationship to last, you want to make your relationship work this time. Primarily, you should be certain that the previous dynamics will not be recreated. Since you already understand the role you played in the breakup, it is time to be a better and stronger partner. You have to take this chance while your man is still awed by how much you have improved to show him that it was worth getting back with you. However, you need to be patient to influence him to change the things that you have taken the time to change in yourself. For instance, you need to understand that physical intimacy for him is key. You have to give him time to understand that as he expects this, he should meet your emotional needs. Since you understand everything better now, you will not take it personally when he is silent, and you will not withdraw your love and affection. Also, you will strive to be open and direct about what you feel rather than leave him guessing. You have great tactics to kickstart the relationship and make him fall in love with you again. We will touch on some other things needed to keep the relationship strong in the remainder of this section.

- **Compassionate love:** Right after getting back together, you might experience intense romantic love full of physical attraction, intense love feelings, and constantly thinking about your partner. However, what keeps you going is compassionate love, which is when you care for your partner and become comfortable with each other. You want the best for each other, and you work as a team. Typically, you are the best of friends. However, you want to ensure that the spark never goes away, so you have to spice things up by doing things each of you love the most from time to time. Look for fresh activities such as sports and vacations that will strengthen your bond. If you are not compassionate with your partner, even the small mistakes appear huge to you, and it is hard for you to forgive. Furthermore, you begin to act like you are in a competition, and no one wants to appear small. This will lead to a lack of fulfillment, and the chances of cheating will begin to rise. Remember that you have different needs, and you have to learn to fulfill each other. Therefore, for you to last forever, there has to be compassionate love between both of you.

- **Commitment:** The both of you should believe in making the relationship work. You cannot expect to last long if there is no long-term goal that you can focus on. There has to be something that both of you live up to for you to understand and play your role in the relationship. This requires harmonizing each of your views about what makes a relationship work and understanding the key deal breakers for each other. You must realize that both of you are in charge of the relationship, and you can either make or break it any time. In committing, you are vowing to take each other for who you are, grow together, and constantly improve each other.

- **Good communication:** Changes can occur along the course of the relationship for both of you. With open and constant communication, you are able to talk about these changes and ensure that both of you understand them. Most often, communication is hard for women, because they often assume that men will read their minds. This is the worst approach you can have regarding a partner with whom you have once experienced the pain of heartbreak. The value of good communication cannot be understated. It opens a doorway to your partner's heart, and you understand why they do the things they do.

We established that clashing values are a major cause for breakups, but this does not have to happen. We all have different points of views, feelings, and desires. For instance, you may have seen people who support different political parties but still live happily as a couple. You may wonder how people who have different values manage to have such a relationship. The first aspect that enables the relationship to strive besides varying values is good and effective communication. Largely, good communication is the basis of solving all the disputes and issues that face relationships. Good communication is achieved by listening to what your partner is saying and trying to reason with them.

- **Trust:** Trust is an invaluable currency in a relationship. It is hard for a relationship to work if it isn't apart of it. In this case, you are coming from a breakup, so each of you may have gone on a date with other people among other things that could have happened. You have to play your part in proving that you can be trusted and more importantly that you can trust. Though you may have hurt each other leading into the breakup, this is another version of each of you and another trial - a different time and place. If you cannot trust your partner completely, then the relationship cannot yet be termed as healthy or mature. It is ideal to be with a person you can trust completely. A relationship that is characterized by trust serves as a source of respite and comfort. The problem with a lack of trust with the person you are dating is that it spreads insecurity throughout all your relationships.

- **Friendship:** Remember about focusing on building attraction and friendship? This is important because friendship is an essential quality in romantic relationships. Those people who marry their best friend happen to be the luckiest people in the world. This allows you to start your relationship on a solid foundation if you begin as friends. In the second phase of your relationship, you had set boundaries, so you did not allow yourself to sleep with him yet. In the course of building a friendship, you engage in different discussions and activities that take your admiration and attraction for each other to another level. At this point, it means that the two of you are able to laugh and/or cry together. You are together during both the bad and the good times. A good partner is a person you can share all your secrets with, ask their opinions, and make them a priority in your life. Your best friend is the person you want to always and forever be in your life. Thus, forming a romantic relationship from a platonic friendship makes it more likely for the relationship to last a long time.

- **Sex:** Sex is an important factor in a romantic relationship. There cannot be a relationship if you are not sexually attracted to someone. If that is the case, then you can only be friends with such a person. Sex is not the most important thing in a relationship, but the truth is it helps in releasing stress and improving your mood. Great sex strengthens romantic relationships, but this will depend on the level of the relationship. It is recommended that you have various things to do to release stress and improve your emotional state of mind. This way, the relationship will include various activities to prevent boredom.

What do men really want in a woman?

There is the understanding that men are merely attracted to someone who is beautiful. Although it is an important factor when a man is choosing a partner, the answers go beyond just attractive physical qualities. The following attributes make a woman more attractive to a man.

- **Deep attraction:** Different men have varying tastes and preferences to what they find attractive. Do not get confused about the aspect of attraction, because it goes beyond physical attraction. Men look at the most attractive version of you, so as a woman, you should focus on becoming the most attractive version of yourself possible. To achieve this, you need to increase your effectiveness, your power, and your options. This entails putting effort into your wardrobe and focusing on feeling good about yourself. Also, it is important to be in shape and engage in activities that make you happy.

- **A person they can share a passion with:** Men are largely attracted to a woman who they can share their passion with. Every man finds it appropriate to share or talk about their passion. As a woman, you need to find out what your man is passionate about. Men spend a significant amount of time in their lives looking for someone with whom they have a much deeper connection. Women who know this put in the time to find out their significant other's favorite subject, an aspect that enables the man to feel like their lover understands them on a much deep level.

- **Respect:** Men tend to search for a woman who has respect for herself and for others. They are keen about what you say, where you go, whom you go out with, and what you post on social media. The truth is that men do not want a woman who is everywhere doing everything with everybody. It seems that most men would prefer a woman who enjoys staying at home and reading a book or watching a movie rather than one who goes out on the weekends to drink with her friends.

- **Intelligence/brains:** Men are attracted to smart women. It does not mean that you must have a master's degree. They want someone who is curious about the world and aware of current events. Men like women with whom they can engage in a stimulating conversation. These are women who use their senses and think critically - a woman who is driving to be successful.

- **A sense of humor:** Men like to laugh, and they are commonly attracted to a woman who they can enjoy these laughs with. A woman who cracks jokes and finds some situations in life as funny is invaluable to most men. Such a woman has an entertaining personality, can help relieve stress, and thinks outside the box - even for simple date ideas. Positive humor has been associated with significant satisfaction in a relationship.

- **A sense of understanding when things are stressful:** Life is full of stressors, especially to most young people as they try to figure out their lives. High quality of understanding is important to men when they are looking for a woman to be in a relationship with. How you handle both simple and difficult situations matters. For instance, how do you react when your man tells you that he cannot afford to take you out on a certain weekend or when he cancels a date because he had to deal with something? An understanding woman looks at her man as a human and will not be quick to react to any situation and instead, take a few minutes to de-stress and refocus.

- **Ambition:** A woman who is not ambitious has low chances of meeting a man who wants a serious relationship with her. Almost every man is looking for a planner and caretaker for the family or a woman with whom they will plan a life together. In the case that a man makes the decisions alone, it means that they are yet to find the woman they want. They want a woman who is visionary and looks beyond today; determined women tend to be committed to achieving all they want. Many men desire a woman who is willing to push forward to have a successful career, to be the best mother, and work on having a successful relationship.

- **Humility:** Most men want a humble woman. He doesn't typically like a weak woman, but rather a person who is concerned about peace and protection. A humble person excludes compassion with others. They have the desire to put their men first, which enables them to establish a strong partnership. A humble woman has the decency to acknowledge others.

Avoiding mistakes you made previously

It will be disappointing to have worked all the way then come to a point where you have to break up again. It may not necessarily be a breakup, but your now boyfriend starts complaining of the same issues that had driven you apart during the last breakup. It will be disappointing to you and even more so to them, because they will feel that you were pretending and they failed to realize it. Since you had already broken up for these reasons, the second breakup may be quick and more devastating. It is important to maintain a positive relationship with your partner. If at all there are conflicts because you cannot entirely avoid differences, let them be from unavoidable circumstances. You can begin by implementing, adapting and improving on the qualities noted above.

You should have a positive attitude and positive thoughts about your partner. Most differences originate from being negative because it is easy to be as such. However, simple practices, such as starting every day with happy thoughts about yourself, your partner, and life, play an important role. You should be the person who looks on the bright side of things, even in difficult situations. Being this way will help you focus on the positive attributes and qualities of your partner. It helps prevent you from having thoughts that magnify minor weaknesses and misgivings. These aspects are tied to bad and harmful behavior in relationships, which is to blame your partner when you feel stressed, betrayed, bored, disappointed, or angry. Remember that, in the case of personal improvement, it was mentioned that you should stop seeing your partner as the one who needs to change. In doing so, it creates a series of unhappy situations where nobody takes responsibility or changes for the better.

From the above paragraph, you have learned that it takes changing yourself to avoid making previous mistakes. Because you had strived to change in the earlier weeks, what you will be doing now is improving and polishing some of those skills. It is of the essence to note that addressing your flaws tends to increase optimism. Your partner will feel appreciated, and this will motivate them to change any negative behavior that they may have. However, do not forget the essence of being vocal about things that you want. It is true that everyday irritations, frustrations, and boredom can make the flame die down. Most of the minor issues in a relationship turn out to major turnoff to the same relationship. You may wonder how this happens; the truth is that it happens because people are not open. Do not be this kind of person. Try to speak out, and compliment your boyfriend on his new shirt, shoes, or anything else. You have to note that pushing your partner's buttons will create an automatic understanding. They too will not be quick to react on small things or issues that they may have with you, because you have created the sense of love and appreciation in them.

Moreover, staying focused on your partner is a helpful tactic to avoid things that may drive each other away. Maintaining a connection with your partner is important in preventing distractions. You may be wondering how this is related. In this case, if your partner is always on your mind, even when you are apart, you will consciously determine if an action you are considering doing would make them angry. For instance, staying up late at night with friends is an act that you will avoid, because you know he won't be happy about this. Also, keeping your partner in mind will help you to stay tuned in to their wellbeing, cares, and interests. Assuming that one of the reasons that may have caused the breakup is the fact that you were unsupportive, the aspect of keeping them in mind will help increase your motivation to want to give ideas and offer any assistance to his endeavors. It is comforting to be with a person you have allowed to occupy your mind, because if you had broken up due to a lack of commitment in letting yourself think about him, it means you have managed to outdo fear. As such, you will find spending time together either emotionally, mentally, or physically is stimulating.

As noted, you cannot entirely avoid differences with your partner. Now and then, an issue may arise that might make you or your boyfriend angry or disappointed. What matters is the manner of the approach to your differences, which means that you have to work on yourself. The second issue that matters is the thoughts, affection, or passion you have toward your partner. Someone who you love will not make you angry over petty things, and even when they have made you angry, you will still have a soft heart to dismiss the offenses.

Chapter 10: Recap - Summary of Lessons Learned on How to Get Your Ex Back and Make Him Stay

The core purpose of the book was to guide you on how to get your ex back or rather how to make your ex want and desire to have you back. There is a saying that matters of the heart are very delicate, which is true, because love is a mysterious thing. As much as it is simple to leave someone during a breakup, assuming that you will go on with your life and never mind about them, things later surprise you. In your life, you will come across many people, some of which you have interacted with. Even though you know that the world has over seven billion people, it is not simple to just leave and forget the person you loved. As such, when it comes to love, it is not simple to just walk away. Most people after a breakup become stressed, anxious, and some even become depressed. However, as a woman, the book guides you on how you can escape being desperate and needy to instead be the best version of yourself and someone who is attractive such that your boyfriend will want to have you back.

The first section of the book sought to establish whether your efforts are worth your time. It is more of a basis for understanding the nature of romantic relationships. Also, it is about your recovery process after breaking up and also self-assessment. It is normal to feel lonely, needy, and desperate after a breakup, mostly because of what you shared with your partner. Some people will keep on begging their ex-boyfriend to take them back, but this book discourages such an approach (review section one, which prepares you for the reality of relationships). Clearly, men and women perceive love, dating, and relationships in different ways. Although there are many points to this, you have to note that, just because you have been having good sex with someone, it does not mean that they want to spend the rest of their lives with you; this is especially true for men.

The starting point in the recovery process has been previously discussed. You have the desire to get your ex back, but you need to face it and look at the reasons why you broke up in the first place. This is important, because addressing these reasons gives you a point of reference. If you are the one who caused the breakup, you will not want to repeat the same mistakes again. If it is your partner's mistakes that resulted in the breakup, then you have to look at them and reason as to whether you are willing to forgive him. At the end of this analysis, you should be able to answer the question of whether having thoughts of getting your ex back is the right thing.

After this, you need to do a self-assessment during which you specifically look at yourself in an objective manner rather than in a subjective way. You need to listen to your heart, mind, and soul to know what they want. Also, you need to listen to your body and actually feel what the breakup is doing to you. An important question you need to ask yourself while doing the assessment is whether you actually need him or if you actually love him. You need to be honest with yourself, because in other cases, it is just an obsession. If the thought of spending the rest of your life with the person does not come into your mind, then you do not need to pursue the relationship. Given all things that your ex did to you, are you willing to compromise and forgive him in order to be back in a relationship with them?

In week 1 of the recovery process, it is noted that you are striving to stop appearing insecure and needy. Feeling desperate and needy are common after a breakup. You love this person, and you are used to them, so the thought of being without them is unbearable. As a result, you feel tempted to beg them to keep the relationship going. Refrain from contacting your ex at all costs. Do not text, call, email, or check their status on different social media networks, such as Facebook, Twitter, or Instagram. You can go ahead and block them if you feel that you will be tempted. Learn to pay attention to other things.

As noted in the second week, it is okay to grieve after a breakup. You should set up a time to grieve, but as you do so, ensure that your core purpose is to become a better person. You need to be a person you can be proud of. It is possible to enhance your mental and physical capacity through various activities, such as exercise, meditation, and even changing your wardrobe. Also, learn to drop the negative behaviors and habits and develop an improved personality. Enhance your communications skills, if you had a drinking problem, drop it now, and if you are selfish, learn to be compassionate. Furthermore, focus on professional or academic performance. Do your best and give yourself a chance to be the employee of the year or to get a higher grade than you have ever achieved. The focus is on becoming someone your ex cannot resist. Focus on personal improvement, and you will build attractiveness.

The third week is about contacting your ex. There are various mediums that you can use, with a text being the most conventional in the current times. However, the main issue is knowing the right time to contact them. A notable point herein is that, if you feel that you are not ready, which means you are feeling desperate and needy, you should not contact him. Take your time to heal and, more importantly, take time to ensure that you have made actual and credible changes. They should not be changes that will wear out the moment you see him or get back with him. When you're ready, you will engage them in a conversation for a certain duration of time. You have to be casual in the way you text. After building trust and attraction, you can then suggest that you go out on a date. There are various things you have to observe, as discussed in this chapter. For instance, do not call the meeting a date, and do not push them to meet you.

During the last week, you are to purposefully meet your ex. Remember the value of having built attractiveness in you. You are well dressed, you have a good body shape, you have developed proper communication skills, and you are no longer needy and desperate. There are various things you should not do during the date, one of which being suggesting that you get back together. If you have made it to this point, then it will not take you long to realize whether you can get back together. An important aspect you should observe is showing emotions, because they may have said something negative as a test.

Finally, now that you have gotten your boyfriend back after they suggested it and after going out on several dates, the concern is now keeping him. You have to know that there are common things that keep the relationship strong. One of these is compassionate actions, affection, communication, and trust, among others. Also, keep in mind what men like and what they are always looking for in women. For instance, a man wants someone who has a sense of humor and who is intelligent, thoughtful, a good listener, and someone who learns how to adapt and improve on these qualities.

Conclusion

The book has offered clear guidance and simple steps that will help you get satisfaction in life by rekindling the relationship your ex. The information you have read is about perfecting yourself such that your ex will not want to let you go again. While in most cases, things do not work out as we hoped, there are certain circumstances where an individual can control things. In this case, you should not let the breakup be your downfall. It is a terrible thing, but you can deal with it, and in the end, you will be a strong person than you were before.

The book placed an emphasis on personal wellbeing. The essence of this perception is to ensure that you have enhanced your inner self to accept things as they come. It is right to state that, once in a relationship, people tend to be comfortable and show little concern about how they look. The book challenges you to use a breakup as an opportunity to be reborn.

You may say that the things outlined and discussed in the book are easier said than done. However, this is something that you can achieve within a short period of time. Remember, you do not need to suppress your emotions so that you can be strong while the breakup is hurting you. It is alright to grieve, but there are measures that you can take to use this to your advantage. You need to be sure that you really love your ex-boyfriend and you feel that he is the one before trying to get him back into a relationship with you. However, at the time of contacting him, be sure that you can distinguish that you want him but don't necessarily need him. Keep in mind that arriving at this point will require hard work. This is to improve your mental capabilities and develop a proper behavior system.

After reading this book, you should now know the reasons for working on personal improvement. One is that you will be attractive, so your partner will find it hard to resist you. Also, you will be proud of yourself, comfortable, and amazed by the person you have become. At this point, you have built self-confidence and managed to address self-esteem issues. Having self-awareness, which you gained in the course of self-improvement, is essential in life. You are now a stronger person and someone who has made permanent changes. As such, you will be ready to deal with the response your partner gives; whether they will be willing to take you back or not, it will be okay with you.

Therefore, it is possible to get your ex-boyfriend back by making them want you and find it difficult to resist you. However, even when you have come together once again, you need to continue improving yourself. You should be aware that differences and conflicts are inevitable in a relationship and what matters is how you resolve those differences. Thus, having good communication skills, a positive attitude, and knowing the right time to argue are important qualities to avoid losing your boyfriend again.

I hope that this book has helped you along your journey to return your true love to your life. If you enjoyed this reading please leave a short review on Amazon. Thank you!

OTHER BOOKS FROM THE AUTHOR

Make Him Beg and Get the Guy You Want

Choose, Tease, Ignore, Then... Catch Him! - The 4 Steps Foolproof Method on How to Attract Men and Make Them Obsessed With You

https://www.amazon.com/dp/B07VVM3FH3

www.ingramcontent.com/pod-product-compliance
Lightning Source LLC
Chambersburg PA
CBHW060424290526
45791CB00002B/865